HOW TO GET UNSTUCK FROM
THE NEGATIVE MUCK

HOW TO GET UNSTUCK FROM THE NEGATIVE MUCK:
A KID'S GUIDE TO GETTING RID OF NEGATIVE THINKING

LAKE SULLIVAN, PH.D.

COVER ILLUSTRATION COPYRIGHT © L SULLIVAN

INTERIOR ILLUSTRATIONS COPYRIGHT © L SULLIVAN

EDITING BY: JENNY BOWMAN WWW.JENNYBOWMAN.COM & ADA GARNER

THIS BOOK IS DEDICATED TO MY CHILDREN WITH LOVE.

CONTENTS

A SPECIAL NOTE FOR PARENTS

How To Get Unstuck From The Negative Muck is an innovative guide for helping your child overcome negative thinking patterns. The techniques and strategies used in this guide are grounded firmly in cognitive-behavioral therapy, which has been shown to be effective in addressing and preventing mood disorders such as anxiety and depression.

There are many great resources already available that will help you understand the intricacies of this approach, thus a thorough explanation of cognitive-behavioral therapy is beyond the scope of this book. However, put simply: Cognitive behavioral therapy is based on the belief that our thoughts determine our feelings, which subsequently influence our behavior. Automatic negative thoughts are particularly powerful because they operate just under our awareness. Automatic negative thoughts can lead us to feeling bad about ourselves and not even knowing why we are feeling this way. Then, when we feel bad about ourselves, we are less likely to engage in behaviors that would lift our mood (e.g., exercising, talking to friends, engaging in hobbies, etc.).

This guide will help your child identify and talk back to those automatic negative thoughts that can lead to feeling bad. It will also encourage your child to practice problem-solving and coping skills that will help in everyday stressful situations.

You will find that your child's confidence will increase as he/she becomes more skilled at identifying and talking back to negative thoughts. It is my hope that this book will set the stage for emotion management skills that your child will be able to draw upon for the rest of his/her life!

WHAT YOUR CHILD WILL NEED FOR THIS GUIDE:

A special journal or diary
Timer
Art supplies

Now Available:

HOW TO GET UNSTUCK FROM THE NEGATIVE MUCK KID'S JOURNAL

An interactive companion journal that includes all of the journal exercises in this book. This unique journal is kid-friendly and features extra writing and drawing pages so your child can practice the concepts introduced in this book!

INTRODUCTION FOR KIDS

Sometimes it's hard to be happy.

Every person on this earth has good days and bad days. But sometimes it can feel like there are more bad days than good ones. We all can feel like this at times in our lives.

So this special book may be able to help you if you begin to feel like this. It will teach you how to say things to yourself so that you can feel better. And it will also show you new ways to deal with problems.

This book will be different from other books you have read. For one thing, it won't tell you what to do! Instead, it will help YOU find the best solutions for your problems. Another difference between this book and others you have read is that it has activities for you to do. But the great part is that there are no right or wrong answers!

Because this book has activities for you to do, you will need a special journal or diary. Make sure it is a journal or diary that is just for this book. Also choose one that you will like to write and draw in.

Whenever you see **JOURNAL EXERCISE**, get out your journal and do the activity in it.

Have fun learning new ways to say goodbye to bad feelings!

WHAT YOU WILL NEED FOR THIS BOOK:

A special journal or diary
Timer
Art supplies

CHAPTER 1

WHAT IS NEGATIVE MUCK?

Negative muck is the stuff you say to yourself when you feel sad, angry, or scared. You don't say these things out loud. Instead you say them silently to yourself. And did you know, when you say things to yourself silently, you can sometimes say them so fast that you may not even know that you've said them? These are called thoughts. And thoughts are super fast! They are so fast that it's sometimes hard to know they are there.

Let's take a closer look at thoughts.

Thoughts are always in your head, but you might not always know they are there. It is just like how goldfish swim in water.

They need the water to survive and it is completely natural for them to be under water. But, they don't even really know they are under water. They just swim.

Thoughts are the same way.

They are always around. The silly thing is even if you think you are not thinking about anything - that is a thought!

So, why do you have thoughts?

Your brain makes thoughts because your brain's job is to keep you safe and to help you live. So your brain is always remembering things from the past. Your brain is also always planning for what will happen next. So your brain is always making thoughts.

What do you think would happen if you told your brain to stop thinking thoughts?

To answer this question, let's do a fun, quick exercise. Tell yourself not to think about a blue dog... Whatever you do, don't think about a blue dog...

Okay, now keep on not thinking about a blue dog…

What happened?

I bet you thought about a blue dog!

This is because our brains are always thinking thoughts. It's almost impossible to stop them. Sometimes we get thoughts stuck in our head and no matter how much we want them to go away they are always there. Thoughts are like breathing air. We always breathe air, but we don't stop to think about it very often, do we?

JOURNAL EXERCISE: IDENTIFYING THOUGHTS

STEP 1: Set a timer for 2 minutes.

STEP 2: Write down EVERYTHING you think about during those 2 minutes. Even if you think, "I'm not thinking about anything." Write that down too. Write down your thoughts as they come to you in your head. Just as you see or hear them.

STEP 3: Look at all of the things you wrote down and answer the next questions:

1. Are you surprised by anything you wrote down?
2. Did you have any negative thoughts? Hint: Negative thoughts can make us feel sad or angry.
3. Did you have any positive thoughts? Hint: Positive thoughts are things that we say to ourselves that make us feel happy and excited.
4. Did you have any neutral thoughts? Hint: Neutral thoughts aren't positive or negative. You will probably not feel good or bad – you will just have the thought.

As you likely learned from the thought exercise, you probably have positive, negative, and neutral thoughts all the time. But, let's take a closer look at negative thoughts, since they are the ones that make up negative muck.

Remember how you learned that thoughts can be super fast? Well, sometimes it can almost feel like our brain is raining negative thoughts.

Imagine how fast raindrops come down. Have you ever tried to catch just one? It's very hard because they come down so fast!

What do you think would happen if you stood on a pile of dirt while it rained?

It would turn to mud! You would get stuck in it and it would be hard to move your feet.

The same thing happens when your brain rains down negative thoughts. Just like you can feel stuck in the mud, you can feel like you are stuck in negative thoughts. When this happens, those super fast thoughts raining down on us can make us feel bad.

This is what we'll call negative muck.

It's easy to get stuck in negative muck when our brain rains down negative thoughts. It's hard to catch just one of those thoughts because they are coming down so fast. Before you know it, you could feel like you are stuck in a mud puddle of negative thoughts. And this is not a good feeling at all.

Remember how we said fish swim in the water but they don't even know it. Well, we think the same way a lot of the time. We don't really think about our thoughts, but we still have them all the time. So sometimes you might start thinking about something that makes you sad or angry without even knowing that you just thought that way. In turn, you may start feeling sad or angry and not even know why you feel that way.

Or maybe a thought will make you upset, but you can't get it out of your head. Or sometimes you might start thinking about the worst thing that could possibly happen. Again this is the brain's way of trying to protect you and keep you safe. But sometimes our brains work so hard trying to protect us that they start raining down these kinds of negative thoughts. When this happens, you could start feeling like all of this really bad stuff is going to happen. Can you think of an example of a time you've had a negative thought, and been scared that the worst is going to happen?

This is our brain's way of preparing us for an emergency. It is almost like a fire drill in our minds. It helps us get ready in case bad things happen.

There are many kinds of thoughts that can make you feel bad. Since thoughts can make you feel something, this means that thoughts and feelings work together. It's almost like they are a tag-team. When you have a thought it gives your feelings a high five. Then, your feelings take off running because of the thoughts. And it doesn't matter if these thoughts are positive or negative. They will still send your feelings off on a run.

Thoughts and feelings also work together to make you behave in certain ways or do certain things. . If you find yourself having a lot of negative thoughts about yourself, you will probably feel bad too. And when you feel bad, you may start to do things differently than if you felt good.

For example, have you ever had to leave a friend's house before you were ready?

Do you remember what you thought?

Do you remember how you felt?

Do you remember how you acted when you left?

In this situation, you may have...

THOUGHT: "I don't want to leave!" "Why do I always have to leave early?!"

FELT: Sad about leaving. Angry with your parent for making you leave.

BEHAVED: On the way home, you may have sat with your arms crossed and ignored your parent.

Do you see how thoughts, feelings, and behaviors work together?

Now, what do you think would have happened if you still wanted to stay at your friend's house but had different thoughts about leaving?

For example, let's say you...

THOUGHT: "I still want to stay, but I really had a good time with my friend today. I can't wait to come back!"

You may have **FELT**: Sad about leaving, but happy about having such a good time away from home.

You may have **BEHAVED**: Like you were in a good mood on the way home by talking to your parent about all of the fun things that you did while at your friend's house.

So, this is how thoughts, feelings, and behaviors work together.

Positive thoughts lead to positive feelings, which lead to positive behaviors.

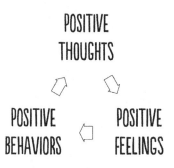

Negative thoughts lead to negative feelings, which lead to negative behaviors.

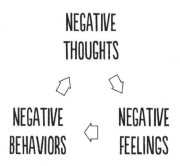

So, when you are stuck in the negative muck, it means you are having a lot of negative thoughts about things that are going on in your life. You may wish that these things weren't happening to you **(THOUGHTS)**. You may feel sad and angry **(FEELINGS)**. And you may not feel like doing the things that you used to do that make you happy **(BEHAVIORS)**.

JOURNAL EXERCISE: DO YOU GET STUCK IN THE NEGATIVE MUCK?

If you were stuck in the negative muck:

What kind of things would you say to yourself?

How would you feel?

What would your face look like?

How would you stand?

What kind of things would you want to do?

What kind of things would you NOT want to do?

Can you name a time when you felt sad about something that happened in your life?

Can you draw a picture of what you looked like? Make sure to draw your face and the way you were standing or sitting. Put some thought bubbles above your head and write in some of the things you said to yourself.

How did you act when you were feeling this way?

Did you do anything that made you feel worse? For example, did you not talk to others about what was bothering you? Did you stay in your room all day?

What did you do to make yourself feel better?

CHAPTER 2

HOW TO SOLVE PROBLEMS YOU CAN CHANGE

If you find yourself stuck in the negative muck, the first thing to do is to figure out if you can solve the problem that is making you stuck. This can be tricky. At first, many problems look like they can't be solved. But once you practice solving problems then you'll get better at it. Then, you may end up solving problems that once looked like they couldn't be solved. But you have to practice, practice, practice!

STEPS TO SOLVING A PROBLEM

First, if you feel comfortable, ask an adult for help with this part of the book. If you don't feel comfortable asking for help, it's okay to do this part alone.

There are five steps to solving problems (see the problem solving chart below):

STEP #1: Write down the problem.

STEP #2: Write down all the ways you could solve the problem (these are called "solutions"). It doesn't matter if some of the ideas are wacky or not likely to happen, write them down anyway. Make sure to also write down ways to solve the problem that would be easy to try.

STEP #3: Go through each of your solutions and write down what will probably happen if you go through with it.

STEP #4: Pick a solution that you think will work best. Ask an adult to help you with this step.

STEP #5: Follow through with the solution. Then come back and write down how well it worked. Give the solution a grade. Give it an "A" if it worked perfectly. Give it a "B" if it worked, but was not a perfect solution. Give it a "C" if it was just okay. Give it a "D" if it didn't work very well, but you can see how it could work in the future. Give it an "F" if it didn't work at all and you can't see how it could ever work in the future.

HOW TO SOLVE A PROBLEM:

WHAT IS THE PROBLEM THAT I'M HAVING?				
	SOLUTION #1:	WHAT WOULD PROBABLY HAPPEN IF I USED SOLUTION #1?	IS #1 THE BEST SOLUTION? WHY OR WHY NOT?	IF YOU CHOSE SOLUTION #1, DID IT WORK? (GIVE IT A GRADE OF A, B, C, D, OR F)
	SOLUTION #2:	WHAT WOULD PROBABLY HAPPEN IF I USED SOLUTION #2?	IS #2 THE BEST SOLUTION? WHY OR WHY NOT?	IF YOU CHOSE SOLUTION #2, DID IT WORK? (GIVE IT A GRADE OF A, B, C, D, OR F)
	SOLUTION #3:	WHAT WOULD PROBABLY HAPPEN IF I USED SOLUTION #3?	IS #3 THE BEST SOLUTION? WHY OR WHY NOT?	IF YOU CHOSE SOLUTION #3, DID IT WORK? (GIVE IT A GRADE OF A, B, C, D, OR F)

JOURNAL EXERCISE: HOW TO SOLVE A PROBLEM

Use the problem solving chart above and try to solve these problems:

1. Pretend that you can't find your favorite hat in your closet. Go through all five of the problem-solving steps above to figure out a solution.

2. Pretend that you lost your backpack at school. Go through all five of the problem-solving steps to figure out a solution.

3. Pretend that you are walking your dog. All of a sudden a car drives by fast and it scares your dog so much that the dog pulls you until you drop the leash. Your dog runs away. Go through all five of the problem-solving steps to figure out what to do.

4. Pretend that you have two friends at school. One day they both decide they do not want to play with you. Go through all five of the problem-solving steps to figure out what to do.

5. Now come up with a problem that you are facing. Go through all five of the problem-solving steps to figure out what to do.

CHAPTER 3

HOW TO COPE WITH PROBLEMS YOU CAN'T CHANGE

What if you have a problem that's making you feel stuck in negative muck, but you can't change it? All of us find ourselves faced with problems we can't change from time to time.

The first thing to do when you are stuck with a problem you can't change is to do something that will make you feel happy. This is called Coping. Coping is a great way to get your mind off of your problems and focus on something else that makes you happy. However, there are healthy ways of coping and unhealthy ways of coping. Let's take a look at unhealthy ways of coping first.

UNHEALTHY COPING

Remember, coping is a way to get your mind off of your problems and focus on something else that makes you happy. But sometimes, people cope in ways that are bad for their body or bad for their future.

For example, if you had a problem and decided to eat a whole big bucket of ice cream because it would make you happy, would that be healthy?

No, it would not be a healthy way to cope.

It might be fun for a while, but you would likely end up with a stomachache. But also, eating a whole bucket of ice cream is being mean to your body. Your body doesn't need a whole bucket of ice cream.

Feeding your body a whole bunch of ice cream would be like buying a huge bag of treats for your pet dog and then giving them all to her at one time. This wouldn't be a healthy or nice thing to do at all, would it?

What if you decided to watch hours and hours of T.V. instead of doing your homework. Would that be a healthy way to cope?

Definitely not.

It might be fun while it lasts, but your grades at school would suffer because you didn't do your homework.

Can you think of other unhealthy ways of coping?

HEALTHY COPING

The great news is that there are tons of healthy ways you can cope with problems.

YOU CAN GET ACTIVE.

So moving your body by playing a sport, riding your bike, or just taking a walk can help a lot.

YOU CAN TALK TO AN ADULT OR A FRIEND.

You can tell an adult you trust about your problem and see if they have any suggestions that might help you. You can also talk to a friend you trust about your problem.

YOU CAN LAUGH.

Find something funny on T.V. or online and laugh until your belly hurts. You can also read a book of jokes.

YOU CAN KEEP A JOURNAL OR DIARY.

Writing down problems in a journal or diary helps many kids feel better about problems they face.

JOURNAL EXERCISE: HOW DO YOU COPE?

Think of a problem you are having and write down 3 healthy ways that you can cope with that problem.

CHAPTER 4

UNDERSTANDING SELF-TALK

When we find ourselves stuck in negative muck with a problem we can't change, the best thing to do is to talk to ourselves in ways that make us feel better. This is called self-talk.

Self-talk is when we say things to ourselves when we are faced with any type of situation. Self-talk can be positive, neutral, or negative.

For example, let's say a girl walks into a library:

If she has **POSITIVE** self-talk, she might say something to herself like: "Wow. Look at all the books I have to choose from! I can't wait to find some books that I will like!"

If she has **NEUTRAL** self-talk, she might say something to herself like: "I wonder when the library closes..."

If she has **NEGATIVE** self-talk, she might say something to herself like: "How am I ever going to find any books that I like? There are too many books to choose from."

So, from this example, can you see how the same person can say very different things to herself because of the kind of self-talk she chooses to have?

Now, if other kids can learn to look at the thoughts they are having and come up with ways to see things more positively they will feel better. Then they will find that a lot of the negative thoughts they are having are not really true.

The same goes for you.

Part of being stuck in the negative muck is having a lot of negative thoughts about yourself, your future, or your world.

You might begin to feel like your brain is a mean teacher who is constantly giving you a report card with all "F's" every day.

It can feel like everything is bad or that you are bad person. This isn't true at all. It's just that you have to learn how to talk back to those thoughts!

JOURNAL EXERCISE: SELF-TALK

Here are four situations that kids often go through. Can you write down what the kids may be saying to themselves?

SITUATION #1:

Paige is playing with her dog, Prince, outside. They are playing with a Frisbee and Prince is excitedly running around trying to catch it in the air. It's a bright and sunny day.

What are some things that Paige may be saying to herself (self-talk)?

SITUATION #2:

Jaden is brushing his teeth.

What are some things that he may be saying to himself (self-talk)?

SITUATION #3:

Samantha goes outside for recess. She sees that her three best friends are using the only jump rope available. They look happy and are stopping every once in awhile to whisper things to each other.

What are some things that Samantha may be saying to herself (self-talk)?

SITUATION #4:

Timothy got back his grade for a science project that he worked really hard on. The grade was much lower than he expected.

What are some things that Timothy may be saying to himself?

CHAPTER 5

CREATING OPPOSITES FOR NEGATIVE SELF-TALK MESSAGES

The good news about negative self-talk is that you can talk back to it! Each kind of negative statement has an opposite positive statement that you can repeat to yourself. This will help you begin to think about things more positively.

Here is a list of negative thoughts and the ways you can change them to be more positive.

NEGATIVE THOUGHTS CHANGED INTO POSITIVE THOUGHTS:

"I'm not Good Enough."

BECOMES

"I am fine just as I am."

"I am not loveable."

BECOMES

"I am loveable."

"People don't love me."

BECOMES

"I have enough love."

"I am a bad Person."

BECOMES

"I am a good, loving person."

"I always make mistakes."

BECOMES

"I do things just fine."

"I deserve only bad things."

BECOMES

"I deserve good things."

"I am damaged."

BECOMES

 "I am healthy."

"I am ugly

BECOMES

"I am good looking."

"I do not deserve…

BECOMES

"I can have..."

"I am stupid."

BECOMES

"I am smart." Or, "I can learn."

"I am not important."

BECOMES

 "I am important."

"I deserve to be unhappy."

BECOMES

 "I deserve to be happy."

"I am bad because I am different."

BECOMES

"I am just fine the way I am."

"I have to be perfect."

BECOMES

"I am fine the way I am."

NEGATIVE THOUGHTS ABOUT YOUR BEHAVIOR:

"I should have done something."

BECOMES

"I did the best I could."

"I did something wrong."

BECOMES

"I can learn from this."

"I am weak."

BECOMES

"I am strong." Or, "I am good enough."

NEGATIVE THOUGHTS ABOUT YOUR SAFETY:

"I cannot trust anyone."

BECOMES

"I can choose who to trust."

"I can't defend myself."

BECOMES

"I can learn to protect myself."

NEGATIVE THOUGHTS ABOUT YOUR ABILITY TO CONTROL THINGS

"I am not in control."

BECOMES

"I am now in control."

"I am helpless."

BECOMES

"I have choices."

"I cannot get what I want."

BECOMES

"I can get some things I want."

"I cannot stand up for myself."

BECOMES

"I can make others aware of my needs."

"I can't let it out."

BECOMES

"I can choose to let it out."

"I cannot be trusted."

BECOMES

"I can be trusted."

"I can't trust myself."

BECOMES

"I can learn to trust myself."

"I can't take care of myself."

BECOMES

"I can choose to take care of myself."

"I am a failure."

BECOMES

"I will succeed."

"I have to be perfect."

BECOMES

"I can make mistakes."

"I can't handle it."

BECOMES

"I am handling it just fine."

EXERCISE: POSITIVE STATEMENTS ALL AROUND

Choose 3 positive statements from the lists above. Choose ones that you think would help you be more positive in your life. Write those statements in big, bold letters on 3 different pieces of blank drawing paper. Decorate those three pages with positive drawings of whatever you choose. Hang the three statements in your room where you can see them everyday.

CHAPTER 6

THE FOUR FLAVORS OF NEGATIVE SELF-TALK MESSAGES & HOW TO TALK BACK TO THEM

Just like there are common flavors of ice cream that you'll find in any ice cream shop, there are four kinds of negative thoughts that are very common for both kids and adults:

ALL OR NOTHING THINKING
JUMPING TO CONCLUSIONS
SHOULD STATEMENTS
MAGNIFICATION

Let's go through each one together.

ALL OR NOTHING THINKING:

Did you know you are an amazing, complex person? But how many times has someone asked you what you did during the day and you said, "Nothing." Yet, if you think about it, we are always doing something even if we are just resting. Just the way your body is put together is amazing.

And your brain is the most amazing and unique part of your body! Our brains are all different. Since our brains control everything we think, say, or do, this means that we all will think, say, or do things differently. So some people will do some things really well and other people won't be able to do the same thing as well. But those other people will be good in something else.

Yet, how many times have you heard someone say that another person is, "Not a good person?" Thinking that a person is "All Bad" when one thing goes wrong is an example of what we call All or Nothing thinking. This is because your mind is labeling something as All Bad. But, usually there is a mixture of things people do well and things people do not do as well.

The same thing can happen when we talk about other things, like sports. We can say things like, "That team is horrible." However, even sports teams that are in last place usually win some games. Or even if they never win a game, they at least score some points. So, no team is truly horrible. They probably do some things right. They also probably make some mistakes as well.

The same is true for you. Maybe you don't do some things as well as other people. Maybe you score last place in something. However, there is always something you are good at doing. And there are always ways you can be helpful even in situations where you can't use your best skills.

This also means that no one is All Good either. No one is perfect. Everyone makes mistakes at times. Even sports teams with the top record have lost a game in the past at some point.

How can you tell if you are having All or Nothing thinking? One secret is to pay attention to see if you use words like: always, everything, never, or nothing.

Have you ever heard yourself say words like this? You probably have many times. You may say things like, "This always happens to me," "They always do this to me," "I'm always late," "I never win," "You never do anything for me," "Every time I try and do something nice for her she is mean to me," "Every time I go to school they laugh at me."

Let's practice trying to figure out what All or Nothing thinking could look like for kids.

JOURNAL EXERCISE: ALL OR NOTHING THINKING IN OTHERS

Michael likes to hang out with his older brother Robert. Sometimes Robert lets him come along when he meets up with his friends to ride bikes. But, lately Robert has not wanted Michael around him. And today, Robert flat out says, "No!" when Michael asks to go with him.

If Michael was having All or Nothing thinking, what are some things he would say to himself? (Hint: Make sure to use words like: "always," "everything," "never," or "nothing.") Ask an adult if you get stuck.

Now, what could he say (self-talk) that DOES NOT use All or Nothing thinking? (Hint: Try to take out words like, "always, " "everything," "never," or "nothing." Instead, use words like, "this time," "sometimes," or "some things.")

JOURNAL EXERCISE: YOUR ALL OR NOTHING THINKING

Keep your journal with you for one day. Pay attention to any time you think or say the words, "always," "everything," "never," or "nothing." You can be in any situation when you think or say these words. Write down what you were thinking or what you said out loud.

Next, write down things you can say to yourself instead without using the words, "always," "everything," "never," or "nothing." (Hint: Try to use words like, "this time," "sometimes," or "some things.")

JUMPING TO CONCLUSIONS:

Another way that we have negative self-talk is when we jump to conclusions. We jump to conclusions through fortune telling and mind reading.

FORTUNE TELLING:

Do you remember the last time you had to stop watching a movie or TV show in the middle? What happened? You probably wondered what happened at the end. You may have even made up your own ending to the story.

We do the same thing with our own thinking. We sometimes act like we know the end of the story when we are only in the middle of it. This is called fortune-telling.

If we are having a good day, then we may make up a happy ending to a situation. We may expect for good things to happen.

But if we are stuck in the negative muck, then we may expect for bad things to happen. We may think that the only ending that could possibly happen is a sad or bad ending.

How do you talk back to yourself when you are making up unhappy endings to stories that are going on in your life?

You stop yourself immediately and tell yourself that you don't know the future!

JOURNAL EXERCISE: FORTUNE-TELLING

Keep your journal with you for another day. Pay attention to any time you think you know the ending to a situation that is happening to you. You can be in any situation when you have these thoughts.. Write down what you think will happen to you. Try to give as many details as you can think of.

Next, write down what actually happened in real life. Notice any differences between what you thought would happen and what actually happened. Take special notice of any fortune-telling thoughts that you had that were negative. Did things end up as bad as you thought they would be? Why or why not?

If they were as bad as you thought they would be, how did you cope? Could you have used any other healthy coping skills you learned about earlier in the book?

If things didn't turn out as bad as you thought they would, what could you have said to yourself to stop the negative fortune-telling?

MIND READING:

Mind reading is almost like fortune telling. But in this case, we think that we can tell what other people are thinking.

If we are having a good day, then we may think that other people are thinking good thoughts about us.

But if we are stuck in the negative muck, then we may think that others are thinking bad thoughts about us.

Imagine you had to wear a T-Shirt with every thought you had printed on the front of it. Would you want to wear that T-Shirt? How many thoughts would be on it? Probably too many to print on the T-Shirt!

The same is true with other people. They also have many thoughts going on in their head, just like you do. So, when you think that you know what other people are thinking - you are probably wrong because you are jumping to conclusions.

For example, you may be looking forward to eating lunch with a friend in the cafeteria. But then at lunchtime, your friend is already at a full table, so you eat with others.

You may have negative thoughts like, "My friend doesn't really like me," or "If he liked me, he would have saved me a seat," or "I was stupid to think he was my friend."

But in reality, your friend may have tried to save you a seat. Or perhaps he didn't think of it, and you had not asked him ahead of time. Maybe he was just really hungry, and only thinking about eating lunch. Perhaps he thinks that you do not want to sit with him. Or maybe he was just thinking about school or his new game at home or a new movie he wants to see — he may not have been thinking about you at all!

How do you talk back to yourself when you start thinking that other people are thinking bad thoughts about you? I'll tell you how:

You stop yourself immediately and tell yourself that you don't know how to read another person's mind!

JOURNAL EXERCISE: MIND-READING

Keep your journal with you for another day. Pay attention to any time you think you know what another person is thinking about you. You can be in any situation when you have these thoughts.. Write down what you think they were thinking about you.

Next, write down other thoughts that they could have been thinking like in the example above. Remember, most people think about a lot of things. So, be sure to write down things that aren't about you at all!

SHOULD STATEMENTS:

What if you had a friend who followed you around all the time and kept bossing you around? No matter how hard you tried to make him happy he just kept getting on your case. He kept telling you everything you should be doing instead of noticing all the things you were already doing.

Would you stay friends with that person for long?

Probably not.

Your brain can seem a lot like that nagging friend. You brain can start telling you all the things that you should be doing.. These are called "should statements."

Here are some examples of "should" statements:

"I SHOULD practice more!"

"I SHOULD make my bed."

"I SHOULD feel happy."

"I SHOULD do this extra credit homework."

Should statements are kind of strange. Because the more you tell yourself you "should" do something, the less you feel like doing it!

This is because should statements can make you feel bad about all of the things you are not doing, instead of feeling good about what you are doing. And when you feel bad, it can be hard to change your behavior.

How can you get rid of "should" statements?

Try saying things like this instead:

"It would be great if..."

"I wish I could..."

JOURNAL EXERCISE: "SHOULD" STATEMENTS

Keep your journal with you for another day. Pay attention to any time you think or say that you "should" do something. You can be in any situation when you have these thoughts. Write down what you said to yourself. Write down how you felt after you said the "should" statement.

Next, write down other things you can say to yourself without using the "should" word. Hint: Try rewriting your "should" statement using the words, "It would be great if..." or "I wish I could..."

Write down how you feel after reading your rewritten statement. Does this new statement make you feel different than the "should" statement? If you feel different reading the new statement, why do you think this happened? Do you think that you felt different because the new statement puts less pressure on you?

MAGNIFICATION:

Imagine a radio station that just played bad news all the time. Imagine turning on the radio and hearing the announcer say, "Today everything was bad. Nothing went right. Nothing will ever go right. This is Bad News Radio. All bad news, all the time."

Would you want to listen to it? Probably not. You would probably shut it off very fast!

But sometimes, we allow our thoughts to be Bad News Radio. We might have ten great things that go right in one day, but we allow our brains to focus on the one thing that didn't go right. This is called magnification.

Just like a magnifying glass, our brains can focus on things that make us feel bad. When we do this, it's like we can't see all the good things that happen to us.

How do we turn off the magnifying glass in our brains? We can tell ourselves that we are focusing too much on bad things. We can also remind ourselves to focus on good things too.

JOURNAL EXERCISE: MAGNIFICATION

Keep your journal with you for another day. Pay attention to any time you begin to focus too much on bad things. Write down what a news announcer would say about the bad things if Bad News Radio was talking to you.

Next, write down other good things that are going on in your life that you can focus on instead. Write down what a news announcer would say if the program changed to Good News Radio.

CHAPTER 7

HOW TO KEEP FROM GETTING STUCK IN THE NEGATIVE MUCK!

When you get stuck in the negative muck you can feel like negative thoughts are raining down over your head. But negative thoughts don't usually start pouring down all of a sudden. Just like rain, they usually start as sprinkles.

So the key for stopping yourself from getting stuck in the middle of a negative thought thunderstorm is to notice when you have just a few sprinkles of negative thoughts. This will mean that you will have to pay close attention to your thoughts and your feelings.

Preventing negative thoughts is not always going to be easy. But just like learning how to ride a bike or tie your shoelaces takes practice, the same goes for this! You'll have to practice trying to stay out of the negative muck. But I can promise you, you will get good at it if you keep trying!

JOURNAL EXERCISE: HOW DO I FEEL?

You've already learned how to pay close attention to your thoughts in this book. So, now all you have to do is practice, practice, practice! This journal exercise will help you learn how to pay attention to your feelings.

HOW TO PAY ATTENTION TO YOUR FEELINGS

Paying attention to your feelings is not very hard to learn. First, take a look at this list of feelings:

HAPPY
CONTENT
NEUTRAL
CONFUSED
SAD
SCARED
ANGRY
DISCOURAGED

Then, every day for the next two weeks, find a time to write in your journal or diary. See the chart below to see how your journal entry can appear. Figure out how you are feeling

based on the list and then write down your feelings in your diary. If you have feelings other than the ones on the list, feel free to write those down instead.

Once you write down your feelings, try to figure out some thoughts that you are having that are making you feel better or worse about what is going on in your life. If you get stuck and need help, ask an adult to help you.

If you are having positive thoughts - excellent! If you are having negative thoughts - no problem. Just go back to the things you learned earlier in the book about talking back to negative self-talk messages and write down ways you can talk back to those negative thoughts.

HOW TO PAY ATTENTION TO YOUR FEELINGS:

DATE:	FEELING?	THOUGHTS THAT ARE MAKING ME FEEL BETTER?	THOUGHTS THAT ARE MAKING ME FEEL WORSE?	THINGS I CAN SAY TO MYSELF TO TALK BACK TO NEGATIVE THOUGHTS:
	HAPPY NEUTRAL CONFUSED SCARED ANGRY CONTENT SAD DISCOURAGED OTHER:			
DATE:	FEELING? HAPPY NEUTRAL CONFUSED SCARED ANGRY CONTENT SAD DISCOURAGED OTHER:	THOUGHTS THAT ARE MAKING ME FEEL BETTER?	THOUGHTS THAT ARE MAKING ME FEEL WORSE?	THINGS I CAN SAY TO MYSELF TO TALK BACK TO NEGATIVE THOUGHTS:
DATE:	FEELING? HAPPY NEUTRAL CONFUSED SCARED ANGRY CONTENT SAD DISCOURAGED OTHER:	THOUGHTS THAT ARE MAKING ME FEEL BETTER?	THOUGHTS THAT ARE MAKING ME FEEL WORSE?	THINGS I CAN SAY TO MYSELF TO TALK BACK TO NEGATIVE THOUGHTS:

ABOUT THE AUTHOR

Dr. Lake Sullivan is a clinical psychologist and university lecturer. She specializes in preventing mental health disorders using research-based techniques.